Forest
Is The Tree Word for Family!

Darby Checketts

Cornerstone Pro-Dev Press
South Jordan, Utah – USA

Website: https://thetreeroost.com

Cornerstone Pro-Dev Press
Division of Cornerstone Professional Development
South Jordan, Utah – USA
Email: darby@customerchampion.com

ISBN: 9798356220456

Printed in the USA.

Dedicated To

All the Trees in the Forests

Acknowledgements

There are many who contributed to this book and other books along my author's path. Thank you, Sharon, for letting me test each new page on you and for your subtle and important observations about what may be otherwise muddled or missing. Thank you, eldest daughter, Natalie, for sharing a practical and a poetic love of the forest. Thanks to sons, Vance & Brent, for being the fine stewards of your respective corners of the forest. Thanks to other dear children, Denise, Cheryl, Ken, Matt, and Lawrence, for your lifelong love and support. My favorite memories are forest outings with you. Thanks to those who read my books with interest and who grasp the "spirit of my intent." Thanks to those who provide the tools and services that make the process of book creation facile and affordable. Thanks to all those who nurture, manage, and protect our forests. Thanks to those who visit and bask in the forests and who do so with loving respect for all the wonders of nature. And thanks to the trees who are the nobility of the Plant Kingdom. You provide the most valuable of resources to humankind so freely and abundantly. You are our beloved partners in making a good life possible on this gem we call Planet Earth. *– Darby Checketts*

P.S. I gladly acknowledge the young "Dwarf Alberta Spruce" tree, who is the newest member of our forest family. His name is Bruce. He recently took up residence in the center of our front yard.

Our Mother Tree Clad in Winter White

- Does a tree have memory?
- Is a tree aware of its own presence and environment?
- Is a tree a sentient being? Does it sense human presence?
- Does a tree communicate with other trees and plants?
- Can a tree communicate with a human outwardly?
- If not outwardly, what would a tree have us know?
- Have you reached out to a tree verbally or non-verbally?
- What was the result?
- What is a tree's value, impact, and contribution?
- What have you learned from a tree?

Introduction

It was June 2015…

Sharon and I walked with John, our realtor, onto three acres in Sanpete County, Utah. The property was covered with Juniper, Pine, Gambel Oak, and a few Cedar trees. There was a rutted path running from the road through the center of the lot. I also noticed tire tracks around some of trees indicating that the property had been sort of an obstacle course for dirt bike and side-by-side riders who lived nearby or who took shortcuts across the valley.

Nearly a hundred beautiful and hearty trees greeted us. We noticed their distinct positions on the property and their personalities. We began to imagine how particular trees would shape the design and destiny of our three acres in the woods.

John led us to a grove of tall, old Gambel Oak trees and suggested these would provide excellent afternoon shade for a picnic area. Nearby, I noticed a large Juniper that had a broken branch at the center-bottom of its wide outgrowth. The gap that resulted between two adjacent branches seemed to suggest an opening for something to be inserted. I immediately imagined a small shed nestled between the two branches. Then, as I looked to the north, there was a tall, broad pine tree that had "Christmas tree" written all over it.

I began to envision how the rutted path would transform into our main driveway. I strolled about to discover other large trees with distinct personalities. Eventually, I discovered a voluminous Juniper that consisted of four very large branches reaching out—each one as a trunk of its own. Strangely, there was a large-diameter center cut where the central trunk of the tree had once stood. I stepped back several paces and immediately envisioned the perfect four-pronged support for a small treehouse. The idea of a treehouse sent my memory in motion and my mind whirling. I moved closer to this magnificent tree. I placed my hand on the largest branch and introduced myself. I whispered, "Dear tree, would you be willing to hold a children's treehouse aloft in the palm of your four special branches?" I will soon tell you of our conversation that followed.

I later learned from one of the wise old men of the valley that the absence of the tree's center trunk was probably the result of an early farmer needing a very long, straight post for a construction project and the cut was made for this purpose.

Already, I had identified a path for our driveway, a place for my first shed, a picnic area, a Christmas tree, and I had found the "Mother Tree" who would preside over our property for many years to come. One-by-one or cluster-by-cluster, nine trees would take on special roles to support the woodland projects I imagined.

This was the beginning of our family's forest retreat and nature connection. We had earlier named our small motorhome "The Owl." It was our cabin on wheels and would be part of the natural "microcosm" we would create over the following years. We called our new rural, forest property "The Owl's Nest." This was not to be a grand estate but a simple camping and recreation site for our extended family. For many years we had enjoyed Utah's five grand national parks, but these had become crowded with happy campers and international tourists. Utah State Parks are abundant and well-kept, but these filled up quickly and had their understandable camping rules to help manage the use of multiple adjacent campsites. We decided we needed a campground of our own. The features of our Owl's Nest would be the facilities of our own "microcosm" campground. [A microcosm is a "small universe" that resembles a larger one.]

There are indeed about ninety trees of various species, size, and personalities at the Owl's Nest. This book will further acquaint you with nine distinct trees who have become special friends, neighbors, and partners. Additionally, there are three trees that each hold a small plaque with these three names: *Michael, Elaine,* and *"PJ."* These are the names of three of our 37 grandchildren who have died but who are ever-present in our hearts. The plaques are in memory of their short lives that blessed ours.

Some of our tree friends are very old. We've been told that many are in the range of 100-125 years or more. The Gambel Oak are deciduous trees. These and the Pine trees seem to be more fragile and short-lived while the Juniper trees are evergreen and very hearty. Our forest is referred to as a *high desert forest.* Rainfall can be insufficient, and the trees must endure. The Junipers know how to do this well. Most of our trees are Juniper, which means that, although we're in a desert environment, our property is blessed with greenery year-round. We have great admiration for our Junipers.

Speaking of endurance, our trees have outlasted many things. There are recurring seasons of drought. Sometimes a drought is followed by sudden cloud bursts that cause flash flooding that washes across our Owl's Nest requiring repairs to the ground cover and the trees that become damaged.

In 2018, Utah had an especially catastrophic season of wildfires. We watched day-by-day as fires raged on hilltops near the town of Milburn to the south. There were helicopters in the air and ground crews fighting to protect our woodlands and the private properties nestled there. We believe that the elevated temperatures and the fire glow that lit the nighttime sky were somehow sensed by our trees. They may have known more of the potential danger than we may acknowledge. Thankfully, our property was not damaged, and our beloved trees were safe.

We had a considerable emergence of Cicada insects this year of 2022. What an amazing phenomenon. The insects did no harm, but their exoskeletons eventually clung in clumps to the bark of many trees and were strewn across the surface of our Owl's Nest. As the short life cycles of the cicada progressed, their deaths produced food for birds and geckos and some fertilizer for the plants. Our trees took all this in stride, including the incessant—yet soft—clicking sounds of cicada that originated in their canopy.

Let me now describe the development of our Owl's Nest and all that this process revealed to us about the beauty of nature and the richness of life in the forest. I will tell you of my relationships with the trees and the reflections on life that I share with them to express the importance of their presence for me and my family. I will describe powerful ways the trees sustain the quality of life on our planet and even help to strengthen the fabric of our human society.

Author's Book Recommendations: This book is about my family's "forest" experience that we gladly share. Our website is a companion resource. On pages 13 and 14, I heartily recommend four outstanding book resources. Two of these, *The Overstory* and *Finding the Mother Tree*, deal thoughtfully and candidly with the true-to-life realities of both *forest* and *human* families including the lifetime challenges they must face. Each of the four books will distinctively enrich your friendships with trees and deepen your appreciation of the forest. The recommendations appear in the order in which I happened to read the books, which proved ideal.

Section 1 – To Begin

Section 1 – To Begin

How Do Trees Rank Among the Plant Species of the World?

Trees tower above other plants. Their combined mass is stupendous. Their **GIFTS** to humanity are almost innumerable to include strong, versatile building material for the construction of essential structures from foundations to rooftops; exquisite material for furnishings, cabinetry, and the creation of many utilitarian and precious items—from toilet seats to jewelry boxes; material for creating tools and implements from broom handles to mighty sailing vessels; the central feature of landscaping for yards and public gardens; and most fundamentally–life-giving and life-saving oxygen, food (fruit, nuts, and more), medicine, fuel, shelter in sudden storms, and shade from the searing sun; AND the fiber to form the very paper upon which this book is printed. Trees are the royal monarchs of the Plant Kingdom. They are partners in our survival and our prosperity.

Who Are the Trees and How Do We Interact with Them?

To begin, here are four books that are highly recommended. These have had a most profound effect for readers worldwide. The four authors are, respectively, the experts on (a) the *sublime science*, (b) the *stories,* (c) the *wonder*, and (d) the *intimate world* of trees.

a) *The Hidden Life of Trees.* In his international bestseller, Peter Wohlleben opens readers' eyes to the amazing processes at work in forests every day. Now this new, breathtakingly illustrated edition, brings these miraculous phenomena to life like never before. It will elevate your forest journeys.

b) *The Overstory.* This *2019 Pulitzer Prize Winner in Fiction* is a sweeping, impassioned work of activism and resistance that is also a stunning evocation of—and paean to—the natural world. From the roots to the crown and back to the seeds, Richard Powers' interlocking fables range from antebellum New York to the late twentieth-century Timber Wars of the Pacific Northwest and beyond. This *fictional* work of genius is rooted in reality–a thoughtful, revelatory adventure that will hold mature readers spellbound.

c) ***Into the Forest: The Secret Language of Trees.*** For millennia, trees have offered renewal and inspiration. They have provided for humanity on every level, from spiritual sanctuary to the raw material for our homes, books, and food. In this revealing book, Susan Tyler Hitchcock joins *National Geographic* to combine legendary photography with cutting-edge science to illuminate exactly how trees influence the life of planet Earth—from our personal lives to the weather cycle. It is a perfect forest odyssey.

d) ***Finding the Mother Tree: Discovering the Wisdom of the Forest.*** In this *New York Times Best Seller*, Suzanne Simard brings us into her world, the intimate world of the trees. She illuminates the truths--that trees are not simply the source of timber; that trees are social, cooperative creatures connected through underground networks by which they communicate their vitality and vulnerabilities with communal lives not that different from our own. The book is a candid journal about the personal dedication required to produce the scientific breakthroughs that transform our world and lift us up.

The paragraphs that follow will address the 10 questions found on page six at the beginning of the book. Please contemplate your own response to each question. Hold in your mind the image of a person standing next to a mighty Oak, Redwood, or Juniper tree with a hand gently placed on the tree's massive trunk.

Does a Tree Have Memory? The inner rings of a tree's trunk mark the individual years of its existence. The varying width of the rings indicates those years of *abundance and growth* versus those of *scarcity and struggle*. The tree's bark and branches are evidence of natural catastrophes, of beetle infestations, of the effects of squirrel and bird encounters, and of human use and abuse. The foundational roots of the tree also mark the pathways of collaboration with other members of the forest community. The heartwood and pith of the tree bear a chemical record of the tree's miraculous utilization of soil, water, and sunlight to enrich its life and make such incomparable gifts to humankind and forest friends.

Is a Tree Aware of Its Own Presence and Environment? Trees constantly assess the quality of the air, the availability of moisture, the level of sunlight, and the contents of the soil. They are aware of all changes to their own chemistry and the atmosphere around them.

Is a Tree a Sentient being? Does It Sense Human Presence? I will let you decide about sentiency based on the plants you know and love. Do your plants sense your presence? They will certainly react to the good or the harm you may do to them.

Does a Tree Communicate with Other Trees and Plants? Through the underground system of plant roots and the fungi, trees detect what is going on within their plant community and the atmosphere. Chemical signals travel among the forest plants at the onslaught of a drought, an invasion of beetles, and perhaps the buzzing vibration of chainsaws.

Can a Tree Communicate with Humans Outwardly? Once when rocking back and forth within a tree canopy, perhaps too carelessly pruning one branch of a tree, I had another branch fall and hit me. I got the message. My fruit trees send me signals when there is neglect. The peaked look of their fruit signals distress.

If Not Outwardly, What Would a Tree Have Us Know? It expects that trees are not taken for granted and that we intend to protect them and use their gifts wisely and gratefully. While they do not feel pain as animals do, they nevertheless do not appreciate abrupt manipulation that damages their roots, bark, branches, foliage, or fruit.

Have You Reached Out to a Tree Verbally or Non-verbally? Each reader will recall their connections with trees. I have hugged and prayed for my trees. I share my thoughts and feelings with them. I lean on them. I sit among them. I ask them for permission as I utilize their gifts. I express my deep gratitude.

What Has Been the Result? If a tree somehow senses my dispositions toward it, I am delighted. If not, my life is enriched by not taking it for-granted. My tree partners at our family "Owl's Nest" are healthy and have not responded adversely to my pruning of them or to the various careful attachments I've made to their branches to support the recreational features of our property. As the wind whispers through their branches and foliage, I detect an acceptance of my presence. It is a constructive presence.

What Is a Tree's Value, Impact, and Contribution? It is the composite effect of the many gifts of trees to humanity as mentioned earlier on page 13 and as shown in Appendix D. At our woodland property in the forest at Sanpete County, trees enhance the fun, the pleasantness, and the beauty of our family retreats to nature. They stabilize the earth beneath our feet, protect us from storms and blaring sunshine, and they provide leafy and evergreen adornment to an otherwise boring, albeit useful, plot of earth.

What have I learned from a tree (the Mother Tree)? I have witnessed these traits: Presence, Patience, Tranquility…Stability, Durability, Endurance…Productivity, Generosity, and Beauty.

A Conversation with the Mother Tree

Don't you sometimes wish a beloved horse or devoted canine friend could speak. We have learned that *animals* are smarter than we might have assumed. Animal voices do communicate. Someday, we may do a better job of interpreting the subtleties of what these are attempting to say. Perhaps it is time to give *plants* more credit for how smart and deliberately helpful they are. Perhaps they have more to communicate than we may hear.

Do animals and plants have a sense of purpose? All living things are driven to survive, reproduce, and enrich their environments somehow. Is this about purpose? Humans understand the vital importance of purpose. Animals somehow have a sense of purpose. Perhaps with plants it is simply about their DNA programming. We talk about instincts that are *ingrained* in a human psyche. That's an interesting word "ingrained." One principal dictionary definition of "grain" is *the longitudinal arrangement or pattern of fibers in wood, paper, etc.* We talk about cutting wood with or against the grain. We talk figuratively about humans *going with the grain* or *doing something that goes against the grain.* What does the metaphor mean? Perhaps what is ingrained in a human or animal is a personality or behavioral trait. It is a tree's grain that guides its growth and accounts for its strength. The grain is a pattern. I think our Mother Tree in the forest at our "Owl's Nest" has multiple purposes ingrained within it and I came along to help fulfill one of these and the result has blessed me greatly.

My purpose here is to honor the natural world and all the miraculous creatures that (or perhaps *who*) live within it. It is not my objective to propose that trees can speak, but to have you consider what they would have us know if they could speak. Here are the words I spoke to our Mother Tree when we first met and the impressions I felt in my mind and heart as I tried diligently to *hear her,* as I experienced her physical presence and listened to the wind in her branches….

Me: "Hello hearty, handsome tree. From what I see and have been told, your center trunk was seized some years ago by an enterprising settler of this valley. The four surrounding branches have prospered, nevertheless. This all could be a blessing to me. The space among these branches appears to be the perfect place to perch a small treehouse for my grandchildren to enjoy. Would this be acceptable to you?"

Impression: "Thank you for your appreciation. The space among my branches is available as needed. These branches are strong enough to hold a small treehouse."

Me: "I will have to put some mounting screws in place, one in each branch. Can you tolerate this? Will you please forgive me if this is somehow an intrusion and painful? The treehouse will not be rigidly fixed to the branches. The treehouse frame will ride upon these screws, which will allow for the needed mobility of your branches due to wind and tree growth."

Impression: "Pain is not the same for trees as it is for animals. If the branches are not needlessly cut-through or split in the process, the screws will be acceptable."

Me: "By this cooperation and assistance, you will become a principal partner of mine. You will serve as a focal point among the other features of this special property. You will be as the *host tree* or *Mother Tree.*"

Impression: "I am honored. I have sat here, growing quietly for many decades. This partnership with you will be a fulfillment of purpose for me."

Me: "Thank you, dear tree. I pray that you will stay healthy and strong and live for many more years as our family's special forest friend."

Impression: "Important word, 'forest.' It means *family* to us trees. Welcome to our family."

Section 2 – To Wander & Wonder

Section 2 – To Wander and Wonder

The two essays that follow also appear at our *Tree Partnership* website, which is located at https://thetreeroost.com. These are offered with this philosophy in mind. In life, before we decide *what to do* and *how to do it,* we do benefit from understanding *why to do it* in the first place. This book is dedicated to TREES and our relationships with them as our friends and as fellow protectors of Planet Earth. I strongly sense two chief *why-to's* (see essays below) for such a partnership with trees. The years of a new decade, starting with 2020, have been tumultuous in multiple ways for Americans. We have faced monumental issues of public health decline, economic insecurity, civil unrest, political turmoil, and catastrophic climate change. The result of these has been to threaten our well-being and to weaken our national unity as Americans. Trees are here to help. Healthy life on earth is unimaginable without them.

Essay #1
Tree partners sustain our very lives
and assure a livable environment for our families.

No plant family is more useful and helpful to us than trees. Their wood is both fuel and our most versatile and beautiful construction material. They anchor the soil and release oxygen during the nighttime hours. Many trees bear edible fruit and nuts. The shade of trees is not trivial. It can be lifesaving. Trees provide a sanctuary to escape the busyness, concrete, and air pollution of our cities.

The A-A-A Challenges: As we observe families, neighbors, workmates, and fellow Americans generally, we may sense *Anxious Minds* and *Aching Hearts,* and we may hear *Angry Voices.* Anxious is what we become when we are afraid or confused. These feelings can be overcome with HOPE and TRUTH. Aching hearts result from a deep sense of loss. LOVE is the remedy. Anger is often the result of being unheard or oppressed. These wounds must be healed through new paradigms of GENEROSITY and forgiveness.

HOPE is reborn with each sunrise. An inner compass points the way to TRUTH. We witness LOVE as we see the Robins feed their hatchlings. Trees show us the epitome of GENEROSITY. They stand firm with deep roots and hold the ground. Their canopy spreads to shelter all creatures. Their breath is the gift of oxygen. Life-bearing seeds emerge each year—some as nuts and fruit. Through amputation and upon their death, trees yield their wood as many treasures for humankind and forest friends.

I go to the mountains, verdant valleys, and the forest to reconnect with all the creative forces of nature. I go to observe the majestic elk, graceful deer, furry critters, and colorful birds of all kinds. I go to see wildflowers and to feel the ferns brush against my legs. I go to sit in a meadow to view the incomparable beauty of lofty peaks and sky-blue lakes. I have read numerous articles that tell of those humans who are nature-bound with the intent to **bathe their souls in the forest**. They walk among the forest undergrowth, beneath the leaves and needles of trees, to let a gentle breeze and the rich aromas of the woodlands wash down upon and around them. Some make the symbolic gesture of brushing their hands down their arms and legs to cleanse and refresh their souls.

Look to nature. My slogan is: *As the sweet forest wind sweeps across our homeland, may we love our nation and our neighbors.* This is the true purpose and promise of nature's creation.

Footnote: My devout friends might ask me about God's role in all of this. I reserve the mention of God out of respect for the diverse spiritual philosophies of humankind. But I must tell my readers that, as I view the stars in the heavens, watch the leaves of the Quaking Aspen trees move, and savor the sublime nectar of honeybees on my morning toast, my reverence for life on our planet increases. My soul prompts this reflection: *A philosopher once asked a person of faith, "Where is God?" The reply, "Let me first ask you, where is God not?"* – Adaptation from: **John Arrowsmith** (1602-1659)

Essay #2
Trees can help reunite us as Americans and strengthen the fabric of our communities.

I propose that trees can be a catalyst for strengthening our physical and mental health and help to preserve our family and neighborly relationships. As we partner with trees to defeat the adverse effects of climate change, they can help to unite us. Together we determine to defeat a common enemy—*the devastating forces of extreme weather.*

[As an aside] It occurs to me that I am a lifelong "Ford guy." I've owned three Ford pick-ups. I worked for Ford Motor Company in Michigan for four years. I recall many conversations with other men (including my own sons) where we have debated the merits of a **Ford** pick-up truck vs. a **Chevy** pick-up truck. Such truck-vs-truck debates may be mistaken or taken too seriously. For instance, "Let me tell you that it's not about *fix-or-repair-daily.* Ford trucks are tough. I helped build 'em and I should know. Okay, I do see some awesome Silverado pick-ups out there." **The point here is:** If we let our disagreements intensify, these can weaken our friendship. We do sometimes let philosophical issues, which may be trivial or not, turn us into *situational adversaries.* Whether we are conflicted over *the* *best pick-up truck,* or which fast food restaurant makes the best tacos, or the ethnic differences we don't get, or the contradictory political ideologies we espouse, these disconnects can make us foes. We may temporarily forget the core values that can unite us. By contrast, when we face a sinister threat to our national security, our freedom, and the safety of our families, we are quickly united and rightfully powerful.

I know there are contradictory opinions about climate change, but tornadoes and wildfires do not discriminate or differentiate between my house and yours. *Our entire neighborhood may be destroyed.* We have watched homes burn in California and Colorado; homes obliterated by tornadoes in our heartland; neighborhoods devastated by floods in Puerto Rico and Florida; and the excesses of winter weather shut down one of America's most vital coastal corridors. In my home state, we have seen the levels of ground moisture sink to all-time lows. Our farmers are digging wells deeper and deeper. I worry about the thirsty livestock and even the Maple trees in our front yard. Utah's drought threatens agriculture and our mountain snowpack that affects the skiing and tourism industries. This ultimately has a negative economic impact for all Utahns.

Great strength comes when we seize the common ground and mobilize ourselves to face an external enemy that is undeniably dangerous to us all. Being together in the trenches of such a battle ignites clarity of purpose and forges mutual respect. My dad was a **WWII** pilot in the United States Army Air Corps (later, the Air Force). He and my courageous mother knew exactly who our nation's foreign enemy was. My parents were joined by millions of Americans who put aside their cultural and political differences to defeat this foe that threatened everything we Americans love. The ***Greatest Generation*** didn't claim to be heroes. They simply seized the moment to harness the enormous power of unified Americans to protect the core values of family, freedom, and faith. They responded as one nation.

This may sound surreal, but I believe we Americans will get past the extended effects of the pandemic, solve our economic problems, remember to show civility toward each other, and mend our political system. In the meantime, we face an immense environmental threat to the quality of life on our planet. The next two decades are critical to our success. Let's join with the trees to fortify our physical environment–to keep it moist, green, and growing.

We need *more trees*. We need the glaciers to stop melting. We need more snow in our mountains. We need reservoirs and underground aquifers to be replenished. We need an atmospheric balance of all the elements. We need less carbon dioxide and more oxygen. We need a mighty army of Americans to protect our magnificent planet. Together with the trees, we can be custodians of our most fundamental business, agricultural, and even social assets–the resources of the *natural world* upon which all our livelihoods do depend!

Instead of spending too much time debating the merits of pick-up trucks, let's get out our wallets and throw our shovels in our trucks to go plant trees. Let's pick up our chain saws (whichever awesome brands we may own) to cultivate and conserve the woodlands near our towns while listening to the trees and *letting the ways of nature prevail*. If you've got spare acreage, plant trees. Contact local forest agencies and conservation groups to get advice and assistance. Let us conserve all water resources and be vigilant about air quality. Let's preserve **America the Beautiful**, land that we love.

Go for a walk in the woods with old friends, new friends, and family. Listen to the wind in the trees and the birds singing. Talk of things that uplift the human spirit.

I am not merely a tree lover though I have hugged my Juniper trees. I seek to be a *Tree Partner*. I propose that **TREES** be symbols of our unity and love of country! I want my great-grandkids to enjoy this planet the way Sharon and I have done. They'll read in history books about the great climate turnaround we made happen. I invite you to join the partnership. The forest family will be with us.

As the sweet forest wind sweeps across our homeland,
may we love our nation and our neighbors.

Section 3 – To Find & Create

Section 3 - To Find and Create a
Retreat from the Turmoil of a Modern World
into the Tranquility of Nature's Wonderland

There are many methods we humans use to escape from life's burdensome problems and occasional unpleasantness. We can lose ourselves in various mood remedies or we can lose ourselves in service to others. I just re-read an article on how to deal with the gloom of the tragically historic Covid pandemic. It suggests, "Just be a helper." Help those who are struggling more than you are and your own troubles will shrink as you do.

There are many philosophic approaches to increasing our level of happiness. Cultivate those that brighten your frame of mind, increase your zest for life, and strengthen your faith.

There is solace in the natural world! There is such beauty in the natural world. There are those who go to *bathe their souls in the forest*. You may think that "bathe in the forest" is a just a figure of speech…but walking among the ferns and wildflowers and among the trees *is* to cleanse one's soul of the turmoil that our modern world too often represents whether it is about work pressures, freeway traffic, information overload, financial worries, relationship struggles, health concerns, or the societal issues that tend to overwhelm us.

My first exposure to *cleansing in nature* came as a youth as I would go camping with my family. As the years went by, our family eventually bought a 20-acre ranch in South Phoenix, Arizona. We raised scrumptious dates (as from date palms) and juicy watermelons. We kept a flock of sheep, a small herd of cattle, and a stable of Quarter Horses and Shetland Ponies. I loved caring for the crops and being around the animals, especially the horses.

Over a half-century ago, I married Sharon. For several decades, we were primarily and happily occupied with rearing our seven children and providing for them. My career led to my life's work as an author. Then, Sharon and I "semi-retired." I had been blessed to have a career coach who taught me the secrets to "re-inventing" myself at the various stages of life. For four years, I served our community as a substitute schoolteacher. I worked for a couple of years in the "outdoor outfitter" retail industry. Sharon and I served our community as education advisors to assist college students with serious financial challenges. We eventually established a scholarship fund to further extend our service to them. I became *re-focused* rather than *re-tired*.

Along the way, we returned to nature. We bought a compact motorhome. We traveled the Intermountain West region of the USA. As our national parks became more congested, campgrounds became more crowded, and RV resorts more expensive, we decided we needed our own family campsite. We created what we affectionately call the "Owl's Nest" (ON). This section of the book describes the step-by-step process we followed to do so. No project before has so engaged my creativity and brought me such deep satisfaction. It is a more feasible and affordable enterprise than you may think. Perhaps you will be inspired to create your own "Owl's Nest." Here are the steps…

Step 1 - Where?
Step 2 - Infrastructure, Storage, and Securing Your Property
Step 3 - An Initial, Portable Cabin (an RV or a Good Tent)
Step 4 - The Facilities and Gear for Outdoor Activities
Step 5 - An OHV and a Barn of Your Own
Step 6 - The Crowning Glory… a Cozy "Cabinette"

IMPORTANT INVITATION: Please visit our Tree Partnership website, which is located at <u>https://thetreeroost.com</u>. You will find numerous photographs that will enhance the following guide to our family's beloved Owl's Nest. Thank you. Enjoy.

Step 1
Where?

My principal geographic frame of reference is Utah where there are many wide-open spaces and numerous rural communities where land is affordable. I am confident that this is the case in every one of the United States. Here is our story. One day when driving home in our small *Pleasure Way* motorhome along what I call the *heartland corridor of central Utah*, U.S. Highway 89, we passed through many rural towns. I love them all. As we wound our way northward through the rolling hills and valleys of Sanpete County, we passed through lovely Manti, Utah, with its serenely elegant hilltop temple. As we passed through tidy Mt. Pleasant and further north, Loafer Mountain was soon on the horizon. It was wearing its fall coat of many colors. I turned to Sharon and said, "This would be a good spot–south and east of the busy Wasatch Front–to create our own campsite. I wonder what property would cost here?" When we got home, I Googled "Property in Indianola and Fairview, Utah." I discovered a realtor who specialized in the area. Soon we met him in the mountain foothills of Sanpete County.

In 2015, we purchased three acres for a surprisingly modest price. The lot was in a secluded area and covered with about ninety Juniper trees and some Pine and Gambel Oak trees. We could imagine our grandchildren scampering through the trees. A shady picnic site was apparent near the Oak trees. As you read on, you will discover that various individual trees or groups of trees became the basis for especially atmospheric enhancements to our new family campsite.

Most of Central Utah is not commercially developed. It is traditional farming country. It is rural and therefore quiet and peaceful. This is not the high-priced land along the more northern *Wasatch Back* as it is called. Property in the areas of Park City, Kamas, Heber City, Midway, and others is more prestigious, but therefore much pricier. These are "bedroom communities" to the Salt Lake City urban and Provo/Orem suburban communities. If you want prestige, you can pay tens of thousands of dollars for just an acre in these areas. As for me and my household, we prefer the lower cost of a quieter back-country environment where rural neighbors count their sheep and cattle rather than their cabin's square footage and how many OHV's (Off Highway Vehicles) are parked in the driveway. There is a side benefit to discovering the more rural environs of central and southern Utah. This accomplishes a needed re-distribution of prosperity across Utah beyond the bustling, highly prosperous Wasatch Front. These same factors hold true in rural Nebraska, Alabama, New Mexico, Oregon, Tennessee, Pennsylvania, Texas, and across the USA. Go buy three acres in a tranquil, rural area. Then discover what you can do to make it a delightful family retreat.

Step 2
Infrastructure, Storage, and Securing Your Property

Our rural property had some scraggly trees in need of serious pruning and some rutted pathways along which water travels from the hills in the springtime and where certain ATV riders had previously taken short cuts through our property. We went to work on the vital infrastructure that a good driveway represents. We soon became acquainted with one colorful, super-friendly longtime resident of our rural neighborhood. He is a rugged and savvy individualist who proved to be a source of much down-to-earth wisdom. He had a small excavator and knew the local sources of sand and gravel. He recommended no pea-sized gravel that tends to disappear into the soil, but rather slightly larger, "2-minus" rocks that stay atop the dirt and eventually form a nearly pavement-like surface. We planned for a wide driveway with space at the end to park a couple of camping trailers and a car or two. BTW: When you are in the "rural" world, you'll meet lots of practical people who know how to get things done without spending a lot of money. And they are often the ones with the very skills and tools that are needed to do the tough stuff us city folk are not always prepared to do.

Next, we posted some no trespassing signs at strategic points around the property just to let the ATV riders know that someone "for real" now owned the property and planned to improve it. We have had no further intruders over the seven years we have owned our special three acres. We have discovered the reality of a "rural rule of respect" for each other's property. It is about, "You don't bother my stuff and I won't bother yours." There is enough space between us and our neighbors that we feel as though we are fifty miles deep into the Juniper Forest. It is so quiet with only two or three cars passing by each day on the dirt road at the edge of our property.

We knew we would have tools, picnic/cooking equipment, and toys to store, so we contracted for the construction of a quality 8x10 shed. We made sure it had a skylight and air vent in the roof. In addition to the door handle lock that was included, I added a "hasp" and padlock.

We put some signs at the entrances to our property and on the storage shed. I found high-quality cedarwood signs online at reasonable prices. We put a chain and no trespassing sign across our driveway entrance. The sign currently on the storage shed is a deterrent to unlikely thieves. It now reads: *"Grandkids'* Barn & Tool Shed." We had sand hauled in to spread around the shed for two purposes--to be our picnic area and to accommodate those who wanted to come visit and pitch their tents without having to deal with any mud. We put in an inexpensive fire pit that consists of the top half of a 50-gallon drum planted in the sand with a lid that assures the quick termination of any fire. Behind the storage shed is a nice wood pile. Since the 2018 wildfire season, we seldom use the fire pit.

Step 3
An Initial, Portable Cabin (an RV or a Good Tent)

We already had a nice compact motorhome that was our cabin on wheels. We had previously named it "The Owl." It serves as our principal lodging when it is nestled in place at the Owl's Nest. A nice travel trailer will also work. We initially invited our kids to bring their tents. Our quality rock driveway made an excellent place to park the motorhome. For the first few years, we just enjoyed having our own campground (or RV resort) without having to make reservations six months in advance, deal with traffic and crowds, pay overnight camping fees, and worry about the "quiet hours" for running our RV generator. Our campground was all ours and so private and so quiet.

The Facilities and Gear for Outdoor Activities

Next, I became an "Imagineer" (like the folks at Disney). I dreamed up things I thought the grandkids and I would like to do. I installed a tetherball pole and a horseshoe pit. I created a safe place for BB gun target practice. We put a briquette barbecue grill in the storage shed along with a *Lifetime* picnic table. As we have no running water, we keep water storage containers in various places. Without permanent toilet facilities, we acquired a *Reliance* porta-potty with its ingenious *Double-Doodie* bags. The storage shed serves a secondary purpose as our "privacy barn" for making use of the porta-potty. We also have toilet facilities in our motorhome. The following are other fun features of the Owl's Nest that Sharon and I created for the grandkids to enjoy.

Owl's Perch: The Owl's Nest was intended to give the Owl (RV) a place to rest. We figured that the grandkids would love an *owl's perch* up in a tree somewhere. I had set my eyes upon one Juniper tree that had its central trunk removed, probably by an early farmer looking for a long, straight post to use for some construction project. From around the center trunk, four branches reached out ready to suspend a special platform among the tree's foliage. I built the perch. It was no easy task, but very rewarding.

There are two folding chairs available at the north end of the perch to accommodate those who would choose to sit for a while. There is a ship's helm at the other end to give children the effect of steering a great ship through the sky. The view of our valley is outstanding and there is always a breeze blowing through the branches to make the perch a comfortable place to hang out. Online, I discovered special "movable mounts" for suspending a tree house that do not damage or restrict the tree. I did a "MacGyver" by going to Home Depot and purchasing various pieces of deck hardware to make my own version of these mounts to save a lot of money versus buying those that are ready-made. There are many websites that provide ingenious ideas for constructing tree houses and for making these appealing and safe for youngsters.

Grandsons' Bear Cave: Five of the most enthusiastic visitors to the Owl's Nest are the five sons of our youngest son and his wife. The boys are currently all under the age of fifteen. The oldest brother was inspired to build what kids usually call a "fort" made from whatever odds and ends may be available. Big brother seized upon a pile of cuttings from my various tree pruning projects. The boys designated their creation as "The Bear Cave." Note: We bought a bear statue at <u>www.blackforestdecor.com</u>. He greets our visitors along with our brilliant American flag.

Picnic Area with Table and Campfire Pit: What is family camping without cookouts and campfires? Not enough. There is no competition for an outdoor breakfast consisting of sausage/bacon, crispy hash browns, fluffy pancakes, scrambled eggs, and lots of orange juice. Okay, French cuisine is delightful. Do crepes instead of pancakes as you wish, but I cannot imagine serving Eggs Benedict and crepes to John Wayne or Clint Eastwood on a cattle drive. A vegan diet can be supremely healthy, but I cannot imagine serving a quinoa and kale salad with soy yogurt to a bunch of hungry ranch hands as Ben Cartwright's guests at their Ponderosa lodge in Nevada (Google "Bonanza" TV Series). Smile.

Sharon and I knew we needed a special new picnic site apart from our tent camping area. We identified a circular grove of large Juniper trees that we carefully pruned to become our secluded place for picnics and campfires. Sharon and I built a "Family Forever" picnic table from the legal logs I cut from a fallen White Fir tree. We added an 11-foot umbrella from Wayfair. Then, we heard grandchild after grandchild ask, "When we come to the Owl's Nest, will we have a campfire?" Oops, our one fire pit was at the sanded tent site and the drought conditions in our high desert forest had increasingly raised the unthinkable prospect of forest wildfires. So, we went to Cal Ranch and bought one of Camp Chef's marvelous propane fire pits. At first our children asked, is it a real fire? The answer is that there are actual multi-colored dancing flames that are hot with lava rocks that glow. An added benefit is that there is no smoke to blow in your face and make your clothes all smokey.

Cookout + Campfire = Family "Nature Connection" Miracle

Tour of Trees: We do love our trees. We created a *Tour of Trees* with a special placard mounted on one tree. It lists the names of our Tree BFF's. This gives our grandchildren the opportunity to appreciate the phenomenally valuable role of trees in our earth's ecology and to understand their importance in adding so much personality to our three-acre property.

Step 5
An "OHV" and a Barn of Our Own

Okay, our friends had them. We wanted some local mobility along the 300 miles of back-country trails and dirt roads that surrounded our property. We knew our grandkids would enjoy rides in one of those OHVs (Off-Highway Vehicles) known as Side-by-Sides (SxS), so we bought a 2016 Honda Pioneer 500. It became affectionately known as the "Owlet," the Owl's baby. What fun it has added. We bought a trailer and towed the owlet back and forth from the Salt Lake City area. The trailer-towing thing became tedious, and it was dangerous on the freeway, we thought. We needed a nest for the owlet, so we designed and then contracted with a company to create a small gambrel-roof barn to further enhance our property. The cost in 2017 was modest, but the cost of lumber has since raised prices. We added an almost life-size "Mustang Horse" image to the exterior wall, cut from a 4x8 piece of plywood using a stencil you can buy online. We tell folks that we could not afford a horse, so rather than have a horse *in* the barn, we would have a horse *on* the barn. Thus, we call the owlet's home, the *Horse Barn*. It has a separate rear driveway with a garage-like, metal roll-up door. It is a secure place for our Honda side-by-side and for other equipment including our electric generator, chain saw, portable Bissel rug vac, etc.

Step 6
The Crowning Glory: A Cozy "Cabinette"

We enjoyed parking our motorhome at the Owl's Nest, but eventually realized that there really was no place for visitors to call "home base." We had a storage shed, picnic area, fun toys, and a barn. Sharon said, "We need a cozy little cabin to hang out in and as a place for children to roll-out their bedding to do easy sleepovers that are much more comfortable than tent camping." Once again, we designed and then hired our barn-builder friends to create a small cabin with a front porch that Grandma especially enjoys. Cost in 2019 was modest (more nowadays). Inside we have a large wool-woven rug, a small maple dining table, a couple of chairs, Coleman cots, and a plethora of throw pillows for lounging. We eventually added a removable "on-porch" facility for using a second *Reliance* porta-potty.

Our cozy, little cabin was almost cozy. It initially had only rough timber showing on the inside until we decided to insulate the walls and redecorate with wood paneling. It is very homey now.

A 2022 Addendum – The Pirates Roost

Ever since building the Owl's Perch, I have wished that it were more of a treehouse—with a roof and some features that would represent more intrigue for our grandchildren. I conceived the idea of transforming the *Owl's Perch* into a *Pirates Roost*. Please let it be known that the pirates who will roost in this new structure are "friendly pirates" whose intent is to do good in the fashion of Robin Hood and his merry band of followers. They may seize treasure from greedy pirates and then share their newfound riches with other friendly and generous children.

In the fall of 2021, Sharon and I set about to add more interest and more fun to our *Owl's Perch* through the captivating *Pirates Roost* enhancements described below.

- **Roof.** We have been watching the world's premier treehouse builder, Pete Nelson, on *Discovery-Plus*. Several of the more rustic treehouses his team built appeared to be beehive-like or bird's-nest-like with exteriors interwoven with the bark and branches in the surrounding outgrowth of their host trees. So, we added a rustic, woodsy roof with cabin-like mini-logs. See the Photo Gallery at our website.
- **Trap Door.** We wanted the good pirates to be able to sneak into the roost undetected and to exit stealthily when needed. It is amazing how much young children like to climb up through and

into, and then back down and out through the secret door-in-the-floor. **Note:** There are trap door safety and security features.

- **Cannon a.k.a. Tennon.** At the window slot on the west side of the roof, we created a turret for a pretend cannon that projects "tennonballs" (a.k.a. tennis balls) rather than cannonballs to defend the Pirates Roost. Greedy pirates will try to invade the roost from the sea to the west. We devised a game where half of the children defend the pirates' fortress and operate the tennon while the others are in an imaginary boat just below attempting to approach, climb, and invade the roost. These pirates must avoid the *tennonballs* or fall from the boat into the imaginary water and be out of the game.

- **Treasure Hunt Opportunity.** We hide a treasure chest somewhere on our forest property and let the pirates follow elaborate clues to retrieve it. This is what they store in the roost that they intend to share with other children and that must be protected.

All this fun and excitement is made possible by our Juniper Forest friends. We have indeed created a woodland wonderland. The northern third of our property is happily called "The Northern Woodlands." The middle third is aptly designated as "Middle Earth." The southernmost section of our property is mysteriously referred to as "The Southern Wilderness." Everything occurs around, among, underneath, or up-there-in the trees. We are immersed in the forest!

Footnote: When you go to *The Tree Roost* website, there is a PDF version of this guide to the creation of our "Owl's Nest" with color photos of each feature of our property. We hope you enjoy. We wish you all the best in discovering your nature connection.

Section 4 – To Fulfill

Section 4 - To Fulfill

The book I wrote prior to this one is *Travels on the American Road with Sean & Vince*. It is based on the travel journals of young, Sean and his 75-year-old friend, Vince. Their stories originate in the fictional town of **Juniper,** named after the Juniper tree. As you now know, these hearty, evergreen trees grow abundantly throughout Utah's **Sanpete County** where my family and I spend much time. In my experience, trees are taken for granted. They are the singularly most useful plants that grow upon the earth. We humans cannot imagine our existence throughout history without them. The trees that live on our small recreational property in Sanpete are mostly Juniper with some Gambel Oak and various Pine trees among them. There are approximately 90 of these and I know each one personally. Each feature of our family retreat was created around a distinct tree or group of trees. These are extra special to me. Here are their names and functions.

- **The Old Oak Patriarchs:** Old Gambel Oak trees that give westerly shade for picnics.

- **Aperta Armis** (Latin for "open arms"): A Juniper with open arms (branches) to embrace the tiny shed.

- **Our Christmas Tree:** A delightfully rotund pine tree that sits silently-at-peace awaiting the holidays.

- **Gnarly Roadside Dudes**: Adorned with knotty protrusions, these provide shade for our motorhome.

- **The Mother Tree:** The generous Juniper tree who provides a lofty and super-fun platform view of our valley and mountains. She is there for all the other trees.

- **Loving Grandparent Trees:** Aged Junipers that welcome the children and bless the family picnic grove.

- **Old Man of the Woods:** A bent and worn, tough old Juniper who guards our horse barn.
- **The Scraggly One:** A truly shaggy, large, aged juniper who shelters the Bear Cave.
- **Cozy Cabin Neighbors:** These Junipers keep company with the cabin guests and help to make a campout sweet.

A Tribute: "Thank you, faithful trees, for the green and colorful character you add to our property…the stability your roots provide the soil beneath you…the canopy of shade you offer us…the firewood your dead branches represent under carefully prescribed conditions…fallen leafy needles that provide a soft and water-proof carpet beneath our feet…oxygen you breath forth each night. And, special thanks to *The Mother Tree* for holding our "Owl's Perch" (now "Pirates Roost") aloft among your four perfectly placed branches so our children can play and pretend as they survey our beautiful valley and the nearby mountains." – *Darby Checketts*

More About Tree Planting and Tree Memorials: Not only do we pay tribute to trees... *We must plant them ourselves to help make our environment more beautiful and health-sustaining.* Plant trees in your yard. Encourage local parks to add more trees. And *trees are a profound way to remember and pay tribute to those we love.* When we (Darby & Sharon) first moved to our current home in Utah, we planted seven beautiful saplings to represent each of our seven children. As another son joined our family, an eighth tree was designated to represent him. Each time we enter our backyard, our children are all represented there. Three of our cherished grandchildren have died, but their spiritual presence still blesses us. We recently dedicated three special trees at our family's "Owl's Nest" in their names.

Epilogue

What about the Mother Tree and her future? This tree is like a mother to me when I'm in the forest where I most love to be. She has been such an outstanding host. She has anchored all our family activities at the Owl's Nest. This family retreat of ours is not a grand multi-million-dollar lodge on a vast estate in the lofty mountains of Utah. It is a placid three-acres in the woods where we can simply sit and relax, enjoy a gentle breeze, read a good book, throw a few horseshoes, pretend to be philanthropic pirates, enjoy side-by-side rides in the foothills, camp overnight, laugh and sing around the campfire, and enjoy outdoor cooking. Not many activities are more curative, rejuvenating, or inspirational than these. We are blessed to have such a place where we strengthened our backs without breaking our bank account to make it happen.

We pray for the safety of our Mother Tree and her community of trees that they will continue to survive the droughts, escape the devastation of wildfires, and know that they are so highly valued by us humans. We love their colors of evergreen and autumn gold, their comforting shade, and the rustle of wind through their branches.

As we re-balance our focus away from material possessions, social media mania, and the perils of politics, we can place more emphasis on preserving the greatest treasure we have: *the natural world around us that is the core resource on which the true quality of our lives depends.* Let our preoccupations be with family, friends, faith, freedom, and the forest.

Appendix Item A

Microchip vs. Maple Leaf

Microchip	Maple Leaf
1. Intelligent, awesome!	1. Intelligent, miraculous!
2. Accesses, processes, and stores digital data.	2. Accesses and processes air, water, sunlight to sustain life.
3. Uses electronic circuits.	3. Uses organic veins.
4. Responds to costly software and endless keystrokes.	4. Responds to soil chemistry and atmospheric conditions.
5. Bugs can be a problem.	5. Bugs can be a problem.
6. Needs external power source and battery back-up.	6. Is its own "photovoltaic" cell, and stores energy as firewood.
7. Costly upgrades needed periodically.	7. No upgrades needed, auto-replaces itself every spring.
8. Patent: IIAWBT Computer	8. Patent: Mother Nature Et Al
9. Requires multi-$B factory and 1000s of humans to manufacture.	9. Requires a free, tiny seed; Nature's nurture; and, possibly, some human protection to grow.
10. Factory is high maintenance with a most-likely negative environmental impact over time. A large adjacent parking lot is essential and a law firm must be retained.	10. The Maple Tree is low maintenance with a positive environmental impact. It is biodegradable and can be repurposed as building material or used as firewood.

Appendix Item B
(Optional)

The Master Forester

And what about a supernal explanation of all the wonder of the natural world? Out of respect for each reader's unique perspectives and beliefs, this appendix is labeled as "optional." I seek a balance between being practically (and politically) correct to not put-off any readers while also being true to my core beliefs. I ask your permission to share my belief regarding the possible existence of a benevolent *Master Forester*–the ultimate *Creator of Trees*–who trusts in a legion of *Mother Trees* to ensure that forest families will thrive.

Many individuals who love the forest may simply believe it to be the wonderful creation of "Mother Nature." This is a sufficient explanation and they're glad trees are here. Others believe the more scientific yet not entirely explainable "Big Bang" theory that trees evolved from galactic dust particles that were somehow transformed into the minerals and substances that ultimately compose tree fiber.

Albert Einstein once said, and it is often repeated: "There are only **two ways to live your life**. One is as though nothing is a miracle. The other is as though everything is a miracle."

The ideas of "creation" and the thoughts of miracles may be superstitious to many. However, there are aspects of the natural world that are so sublime that it might be "too intellectually detached" to dismiss such ideas out of hand. Perhaps there is something that transcends the idea of evolution. Perhaps there is a manifestation of intelligence that transcends sophisticated scientific theories and earnest theologies. I cannot consider the complexity of nature and the useful aspects of a tree without being humbled to the point of saying,

"I cannot prove that God invented trees, but I for sure *cannot* say these are somehow a fortunate accident of nature that resulted from a Big Bang and then millions of years of evolution." There is more to it.

Trees had a VERY early beginning on earth and had to precede other life forms so that their existence would be feasible. Was the availability of firewood an accident of nature that coincidentally allowed early humans to make it through the winter? Early cart builders were thankful that something (or someone) intelligent knew that wooden wheels would be more manufacturable and functional than the round stones they used initially. The total ecosystem effects of trees are profound. To not see the intricacy of the existence of trees for the benefit of other planetary life forms including humans would appear to be ungrateful.

What then is the magnificent *essence* of our world and our universe? All human logic, theories, and beliefs cannot explain it, but we experience the awe. To share my intrigue in writing this appendix, please review the key words, phrases, and ideas on the following page. The ultimate explanation of our wondrous existence *as humans living on our planet gem–delicately balanced among the stars–within a forest family of trees* needs to consider all these possibilities. ⇨

What is the ESSENCE of the wondrous existence of humans living on a planet gem–delicately balanced among the stars–within a forest family of trees?

Darby Checketts Listens to a Majestic Cottonwood at Fruita, Utah

Appendix Item C

(Optional)

The Language of Trees

The theoretical notions I will outline below may be purely fanciful and not bear any accuracy, but the result of contemplating such possibilities could lead to a more benevolent relationship between the tree and the human. Hugging the tree and talking to the tree will increase a human's respect for the tree. Perhaps one of the best reciprocal hugs you can get from a tree is to sit by a campfire on a cold fall night and feel the warmth of logs burning and to gaze at the glowing embers. That's a conversation with a tree.

So, how might a tree communicate in its own vernacular or be interpreted to speak in our language? What impressions might we get?

A. **Tree Speaks.** It could convey a limited number of somewhat vague expressions transmitted as sounds and movements.
B. **Tree Transmits.** In a human language, its communication could be brief thoughts, unspoken, yet discernible as verbal impressions within a human's mind, as prompted by the tree's movement and sounds.
C. **Human Infers.** The human might reasonably infer what the tree *would communicate* if it could do so in a human way.

With possibility "A," what might be the tree sounds (versus words) with meaning?

- Creaking sounds, like wooden floorboards.
- Increased rustling of branches and leaves.

- Sudden stillness.
- Something unexpectedly falling from the tree, e.g., a branch, a fruit, a nut, a seed form—especially if these fell in peculiar ways or places and/or with unusual force.

With possibility "B" expressions, what could be some examples of tree communication?

- "I am pleased" – An "Umm" or soft moaning sound radiating to inside the human head to express the tree's satisfaction.
- "I am displeased" – Creaking sounds to express the tree's dissatisfaction.
- "I am angry" – A vibration or rumbling sound as if coming from the roots.
- "Please listen to me" – A sudden, strong rustling of branches and leaves as with a burst of wind, then with a sudden stop.
- "Look around you to see something important" – A slight yet distinct twisting of the tree in a particular direction.
- "Beware of coming danger" – The abrupt breaking and falling of a branch.
- "I like you" – Fruit or seed forms gently fall at the feet of the human.

The "A" *sounds* would create "loose" impressions and could then become more distinct to be the clues to specific "B" human-like expressions in words. The "C" inferences would be an intuitive sense of what the tree might wish it could say. Think to yourself, "If I were a tree, what would I want to say to my human friend?"

Appendix Item D

Tree Gifts…
To Bless Humanity and the Forest Family

- Strong, versatile building material for the construction of essential structures from their foundations to walls to rooftops,
- Exquisite material for furnishings and cabinetry,
- The basis of many utilitarian and precious items–from toilet seats to jewelry boxes to musical instruments,
- Material for creating tools and implements from broom handles to mighty sailing vessels,
- The central features of landscaping for yards and public gardens,
- Life-giving oxygen (as carbon dioxide is removed from the air),
- Food (fruit, nuts, sap, and more),
- Medicine,
- Invaluable firewood fuel, forest fodder, and rich compost,
- Shelter in sudden storms,
- Shade from the searing sun,
- The essential fiber to form the very paper upon which this book is printed…and to create cardboard shipping cartons,
- Expansive root systems to hold the forest floor firm,
- Mighty trunks and branches as a home to many animals; and available to support treehouses, lookout posts, bird nests, tire swings, rope ladders, zip lines, and to *just climb up*,
- And more. Please add other gifts of which you are aware.

An Opportunity...

We value our family relationships. We want the best for each other and to stay close to one another. This is not always easy to accomplish. There are many distractions in our modern world. With all that is human made, it is surely meaningful to note that the foundation of our lives is built on "natural" things. The natural elements within the earth make everything possible. This paper my book is printed on is essentially tree fiber. Most electric cars run on batteries made from the lithium found buried in the deserts of Asia and South America. Your cell phone is made of plastic from a base petroleum substance stored deep inside the earth millions of years ago. Of course, our food comes from the earth directly or indirectly.

In an oftentimes "virtual world," it benefits our families to know and appreciate natural things. It is so fundamental to take your family to the forest, to drive through the rural countryside on your way and see the cows grazing next to the cornfields where tortilla chips originate. In the forest, look closely for wildlife. Hear the birds. Pick up a pinecone and examine the amazing seed-tech packaging system it represents. Notice the absence of road noise. Listen to the wind in the trees that whispers "all is well."

Take Your Family to the Forest.
Forest is the *Tree Word* for Family.

If there is no forest where you live, go to a forest nearby and/or plant two or three trees where you live that a forest may be there one day.

My Tree Partners

Tree Type:

Tree Location:

Admirable Tree Characteristics:

How I Reach Out to and Encourage the Tree:

The Value of the Tree to Me:

Tree Type:

Tree Location:

Admirable Tree Characteristics:

How I Reach Out to and Encourage the Tree:

The Value of the Tree to Me:

Tree Type:

Tree Location:

Admirable Tree Characteristics:

How I Reach Out to and Encourage the Tree:

The Value of the Tree to Me:

My Nature Connections

Where?

With Whom?

Memorable Experiences:

Results / Take-Away Learning and Commitments:

Where?

With Whom?

Memorable Experiences:

Results / Take-Away Learning and Commitments:

Where?

With Whom?

Memorable Experiences:

Results / Take-Away Learning and Commitments:

General Notes / Inspiration

"I only went out for a walk and finally concluded to stay out till sundown, for going out, I found, was really going in." – *John Muir*

"We need to demonstrate our acceptance of the natural world, including ourselves; we need the spiritual refreshment that being natural can produce." – *Wallace Stegner*

Personal Reflections

Tree Knowledge & Tree Conversations

Oh, Tree House!

What is it about a treehouse? When you climb up, you can almost touch the sky. You can see forever. The branches of the tree hold you. You will hope bears can't get you, but you should still close the door. Some bears can climb. If there are suspicious invaders, you will see them first. You'll feel the breeze in the treetops but not the cold or wet earth below. You can hold secret meetings to plan your adventures. If you have a trap door, you can sneak in or sneak out.

**What Do Members of *Forest*
and *Human* Families Have in Common?**

They stand together
to enhance their durability and beauty.
Their roots give them stability.

Their roots and canopies are intermingled.
They are interdependent.
They know that the success or failure
of a single member affects them all.

Calamities affect them collectively:
violent weather, drought, floods,
beetle infestations, wildfires,
careless campers,
and avaricious harvesters.

They communicate helpful information
and warnings to each other—
trees via fungi and soil chemistry,
humans via their language.

They enjoy birds.

Darby & Sharon Checketts

Darby & Sharon Checketts live in Salt Lake County, Utah. They own a small family retreat in Sanpete County, Utah. Darby is a retired business consultant. After 17 years in the corporate world, he and Sharon established a family-owned business, which they managed for 27 years. Theirs is a large and active posterity, which is the center of their attention these days. Darby is the author of 18 books including his best-selling business book, *Customer Astonishment: 10 Secrets to World-Class Customer Care*. Other books highly relevant to your nature connection are: *The Utah Cure: Three Days & Two Nights, Travels on the American Road with Sean & Vince,* and *The New American Prosperity,* which is a collection of 39 essays to help you deal with life's perplexities and to seize life's amazing possibilities. Darby Checketts' books are available at **Amazon.com**.

Contact...

Darby Checketts
Cornerstone Pro Dev Press
South Jordan, Utah 84095

Please Visit Our Tree Partnership Website.
It is *The Tree Roost* at: https://thetreeroost.com

Inquire at: darby@customerchampion.com

Thank you!